A greatness in profusion

In 1972 the Norfolk Society, from which four years later The Norfolk Churches Trust was to emerge, published a slim book entitled **Norfolk Country Churches and the Future**. *It brought together a distinguished circle of writers and illustrators.* **John Betjeman** *wrote a foreword of poetical eloquence whose words are as apposite now as they were then. In this 25th anniversary book of The Norfolk Churches Trust, as we look forward into the 21st century, we reprint his words in tribute to the man who recognised our churches for the treasure that they are.*

Norfolk is one of the great architectural treasures of Europe because of its medieval country churches. Their *profusion* is their greatness. There are 659 of them.

Some are miracles of soaring lightness with wooden angels in their high up roofs: some have painted screens, or Georgian box pews, or medieval carved bench ends or ancient stained glass. Each is different from its neighbour, even if it is less than a mile off or in the same churchyard. None is without a treasure of some sort in wood, stone, iron, tile or glass. Some are famous throughout Britain. Lovers of the Norfolk churches can never agree which is the best. I have heard it said that you are either a Salle man or a Cawston man. Others say that Walpole St. Peter bears the palm.

Norfolk would not be Norfolk without a church tower on the horizon or round a corner up the lane. We cannot spare a single Norfolk church. When a church has been pulled down the country seems empty or is like a necklace with a jewel missing. Every Norfolk church that is left standing today, however dim, neglected or forgotten it looks, is loved by someone otherwise it would have disappeared long ago.

Norfolk is a faithful county to have kept so many of its churches standing through the centuries. Like St. Mary Magdalene, it has not suggested selling its precious gift to give to the poor, but has known the true value of witness to the faith. God save the Norfolk parish churches. In saving them, we will keep Norfolk the treasure for the future that it is today.

Little Snoring St Andrew. Drawing by Hugh Holbeach

Treasure for the Future
A Celebration
The Norfolk Churches Trust
1976–2001

Edited by

CHARLES ROBERTS

Designed by Mike Fuggle

St Peter's church window in Aldborough St Mary.
Designed by Whitefriars Glassworks, echoing the words of Jesus:
"Thou art Peter, and upon this rock I will build my church, and the
gates of hell shall not prevail against it" Matt.16.18

The Norfolk Churches Trust

Ancient crafted door handle from Ashwellthorpe All Saints.
Photo: Richard Tilbrook

ISBN 0-9502838-6-X

Published by The Norfolk Churches Trust
9 The Old Church, St Matthews Road, Norwich NR1 1SP
Telephone 01603 767-576

Printed by Norwich Colour Print Ltd

Contents

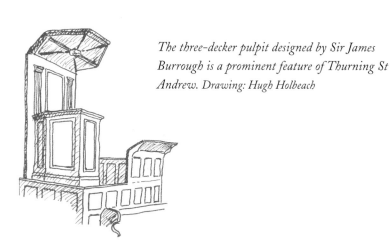

The three-decker pulpit designed by Sir James Burrough is a prominent feature of Thurning St Andrew. Drawing: Hugh Holbeach

ST. JAMES'S PALACE

Norfolk is blessed with some of the finest medieval churches in the country. Their number and magnificence have long provided a welcome sight to native and visitor alike.

The Norfolk Churches Trust has played a significant part, over the past 25 years, in helping to ensure that these splendid buildings remain as churches. From small beginnings the Trust has handed out over £3 million in grants towards the upkeep and conservation of Norfolk's Churches.

The fight to save Norfolk's Churches is one which has found increasing support and triumphed over earlier opposition. The Norfolk Churches Trust has played an important part in this change of attitude and we owe a huge debt of gratitude to Lady Harrod for her unceasing dedication to a very important cause. I am extremely proud to be the Patron of such a successful organisation.

Founder's Reflections

She has been called, affectionately and admiringly, "the patron saint of Norfolk's churches". Lady Harrod founded the Norfolk Churches Trust. A quarter century on, indomitable and inspirational as ever, she is the Trust's president, and still its guiding light.

I have been having great fun looking through 25 years of the Trust's scrap books and news letters; fun because the situation was so bleak in the early '70s compared with nowadays.

The media have nearly always been helpful and supportive to us, but in the 1970s some headlines were not entirely so, like one in the *Sunday Express*: "Vicar tells 4000 - Don't help church appeal" (this was in Berkshire, not Norfolk).

But the general picture was unavoidable: "Many fine churches in dire straits," *EDP*. "Problem of unwanted churches," *Evening Star, 1973*. "Redundancy for thousands of parish churches," *Evening Standard, May 25, 1972*. "Shut church move angers villagers," *EDP, September 29, 1972*. This sort of thing went on and on into 1974 and 1975, but gradually there came a change and the news gets better: "House of God saved from dereliction," *EDP, October 22, 1975*. "Fight to keep church going," (Wilby), *EDP, September 1976*. "Fifty years of devotion," *EDP, September 9, 1976*. "The Church Restored," *Norwich Churchman, April 1976*.

So, rather slowly, but surely, the tide turned. The clergy, from the Bishop downward, began to see that the people did still like to worship in their own familiar churches; and that money was available when really wanted, even though it might be a bother to collect.

But not always! Sometimes the collecting is fun. Witness the marvellous fetes and auctions generously put on for us by Bryan Hall in his treasure house at Banningham. Or the annual Bicycle Ride early in September, so popular that we topped £100,000 last year.

Or the snowdrop mornings; or the endlessly popular flower festivals; the concerts in churches; the crab suppers and so on. Never a dull moment.

And still the money comes in. From the £300 we borrowed in the 1970s from the Norfolk Society (the county branch of the Council for the Protection of Rural England), our accounts this year show that £3,000,000 has passed through our hands in those 25 years. It has helped churches to survive which were almost extinct. I think of places like Wilby, Alby, Cockthorpe, West Rudham and nearly 20 more. At the same time we were able to encourage others who were plodding gamely along, and cheerfully keeping going the C of E in the County of Norfolk.

So down with doom and gloom, which are really only there if you want them to be. Think instead of how many good friends we have, and how lucky we are. Lucky too in that we have always had excellent and enthusiastic people on our committee, and in our office.

There are 659 medieval churches in Norfolk, so we shall have plenty to occupy us and keep us happy in the next 25 years, until we reach another anniversary.

Above Lady Harrod with former Bishop of Norwich the Rt. Revd. Peter Nott

Initial decoration: Carved bench end giving the date and initials of the donor. Cockthorpe St Andrew and All Saints

Worstead Church 1847. Brown wash drawing by A.N. Rolfe.
© *Norwich Castle Museum and Art Gallery*

A voice heard in many different ways

Within mere weeks of Bishop Graham's arrival amongst us as our new Bishop of Norwich, the word went out across the diocese – A warm, approachable man, eloquently clear in his views and his expressions of them, a man who speaks to us all. These qualities shine through in his introductory essay to this 25th anniversary book of The Norfolk Churches Trust

'Stone has a turn for speech'

So begins a poem by U A Fanthorpe about an ancient church. I've thought of it on a good many occasions when lost for adequate words on encountering Norfolk churches for the first time. The stones of so many of our churches speak volumes. They seem to say different things to different people. Some put them firmly into that neat category called heritage. Too neat, perhaps.

Our largest churches are reminders of the grandeur and majesty of God. Sometimes they can be forbidding. But the fear of God is not meant to be frightening. It is about awe and wonder.

Our smaller churches may remind us of God's intimacy, telling us that He inhabits even the small world in which you and I live. A few are genuinely disturbed by these symbols of past wealth, and wonder what the poor made of it all when these churches were built. But it was sometimes the poor who built them. Yes, stones have a turn for speech. There's no doubt about that.

What takes my breath away is the scale of the aspirations of those who built so many Norfolk churches in past generations. These were not people with an impoverished view of the world, but people of extravagance, ingenuity, flair and imagination. These were people captured by the spirit of God, whom they did not domesticate and tame, as we are wont to do.

Far from perfect

They weren't perfect. Far from it. They simply went in for rather different sins to the ones we commit, and so we are liable to think ourselves better than them. That's a failing of our present age - to think we are morally superior to those who have gone before us. Perhaps that's true in every age, only we do not know, since we can only live in our own.

One of the surprising things about our secular times is that cathedrals and parish churches are more visited than ever. When I am at home I say morning prayer in the cathedral with the Dean and Chapter (and generally a few others in the congregation) at 7.30am each day. Every day that service is followed by Holy Communion at 8.00am with a larger congregation, and by the time that service is concluded, the visitors have arrived.

The very scale of the cathedral allows a degree of anonymity. You can enter the building without being thought 'religious' which is clearly the most terrible thing of which to be accused nowadays. The number of people who begin a conversation with me by saying "I'm not religious . . . " is legion. Perhaps they think it protects them from my converting instinct, but all it does is arouse it! I am more practised in observing people visiting the cathedral than I am our parish churches. But I suspect the impact is much the same. The impact is different from a visit to a museum or art gallery or a concert hall. It isn't like visiting a ruined castle or a stately home.

So what is it about churches that draws people to visit them in unprecedented numbers in an age which is not church-going? Why is it we have become a church-visiting nation rather than a church-going people?

Best seller

The best selling book by Simon Jenkins, England's Thousand Best Churches, gives us a clue to the answer in his introductory essay. He sees churches as "memory in stone" and he says it is "through the churches of England that we learn who we were, and thus who we are and might become." He describes them as a "Museum of England". He longs for them to be used for community purposes, and praises those (like Blakeney in our own county) that are models of welcome, and of community spirit, and a delight to the eyes and heart.

What he does not recognise is that he has chosen to visit England's finest church buildings, whereas if he had visited England's least attractive churches, he would have found them adapted for community purposes much more frequently and much more easily.

Frankly, the conservation lobby, thankful though I am for its eagerness for our heritage, can also be a deadening hand where creative use of our church buildings is concerned. We tend to preserve what the last generation left us, rather than re-creating the flexibility with which our medieval ancestors often used their churches.

Simon Jenkins says that our churches are "shrines to the memory of faith". There is a wistfulness in the way in which he writes. He is candid in confessing that the Christian faith is not alive in the present for him, but if our parish churches are simply symbols of the memory of a lost faith, I think they would be sad buildings, leaving people depressed about the unbelief in which they are trapped.

I believe that our church visiting age is one of longing, a longing for faith, and I doubt if our churches would be so rewarding to visit if they were simply a reminder of what we have lost. It's clear that for many their visits to our parish churches and cathedrals are life giving experiences rather than occasions of grief.

Tourist churches

One of the duties I most enjoyed during my first year as Bishop of Norwich was giving the awards for the Norfolk Tourist Church of the Year competition. I believe there were a record number of entries, a reminder that an increasing number of our churches are open to visitors every day. (I wish they were all open, but I do understand the problems.)

One of the features of some of our most popular tourist churches is that they have places where people can leave their prayer requests or light a candle or both. Every day in the cathedral the celebrant at the early morning celebration of Holy Communion finds a pile of cards on his vestments.. These are the requests for prayer from visitors on the previous day. He has to include them in the intercessions because we promise everyone who makes a request that we will pray for them.

So every day we pray by name for adult children with whom parents have lost touch; those afflicted by addiction to drugs or alcohol or both; and those who are bereaved. We pray in thanksgiving for reunions with long lost relatives, or delight in the birth of a child. Sometimes our prayers are for other parts of the world where people long for peace, such as in the land which Jesus of Nazareth knew himself.

Vivid reminder

Many of the prayer requests come from people who express themselves in ways that indicate they are not regular church-goers, but who long for the community of faith which worships in that building to pray for them. It is a vivid reminder that people have a longing to pray and a desire to be prayed for. "Stone has a turn for speech" and the speech is often prayer.

I believe that one of the problems we face in our own age is an extremely narrow understanding of the nature of the Church. In one of her novels Susan Hill describes the feelings of a young woman whose husband has just been killed. She is at his funeral. The author describes her feelings:

She became aware not of the presence of the village people sitting or kneeling behind her, but of others; the church was full of all those who'd ever prayed in it, the air was crammed and vibrating with their goodness, and the freedom and power of their resurrection; and she felt herself to be part of some great living and growing tapestry, every thread of which joined with and crossed and belonged to every other, though each was also entirely and distinctly itself. Is this fanciful? I think not. It is reality that we do not consider sufficiently frequently.

The walls of our churches open out upon eternity. The worship that we offer now is one and the same with the great liturgy of heaven. We need a sense of spiritual solidarity across the generations and down the ages, linking heaven and earth. The Church is not composed simply

Cley Church. Watercolour by James Bulwer. © Norwich Castle Museum and Art Gallery

of those who are living now. That is a worldly vision of the church and it is a besetting sin of our age.

Our churches are a reminder of a community of faith which includes both the living and the departed. What in times past we would have called the Church Militant and the Church Triumphant.

Understanding

It is this understanding of the Church which our ancient church buildings assist us to understand, if we only interpret them in the light of Christian faith. They are not a memory of a faith that has died. They are a sign of a God that still lives. They are reminders of the communion of saints.

God's existence is not subject to democratic vote. The whole human world could cease to believe in Him, but that would not abolish His love or care or forgiveness for our foolishness. As it is, it is only the spiritually deaf and blind western world that has a crisis of faith.

It is because of all this that I believe the work of the Norfolk Churches Trust is so important. We cannot allow the spiritual shortcomings of our own age to deaden our spiritual senses. All that the Norfolk Churches Trust does in supporting our churches is to enable God to speak still through the stones. His voice is heard in many different ways.

"Stone has a turn for speech."

+ Graham Norvic:

11

Barmer All Saints. Specially drawn for Norfolk Country Churches and the Future *by Sir Osbert Lancaster*

Cash, scrubbing brushes and unstoppable zeal

Charles Roberts tells the story of the first 25 years in the life of
The Norfolk Churches Trust

It is difficult to believe that in the 1970s, only a generation ago, the future of many of our medieval churches in Norfolk was in the balance. Congregations were low, clergy were thin on the ground. So the popular attitude was - Close the least used churches, make them redundant, and if necessary, demolish them.

This wave of opinion started in Norwich, rather than in the rural county. In 1967 Bishop Launcelot Fleming appointed a commission led by Lord Brooke of Cumnor, to advise the diocese on the future of the city's remarkable total of 32 medieval churches, more than in any other city in western Europe,

The Commission came to a momentous conclusion - that 24 of these churches "would seem no longer to be required for Church of England parish use". More than three decades on, only a handful of them are alive and open for worship. All but one of the rest have found alternative uses.

Lady Harrod, who a few years later would found The Norfolk Churches Trust, dubbed this proposition as "frightening", and with others she set up a committee whose members called themselves The Friends of Norwich Churches. Looking back, one senses that the Corporation of Norwich was not best pleased with all these county people stepping in and, seemingly, interfering with city affairs. So the city took on the job itself.

"We decided then that we would look after the rural county and its churches", recalls Lady Harrod, "which again seemed a very frightening prospect." As well it might, with 659 medieval churches in Norfolk. Yet when the word went out, many people quickly pledged their keen interest and support.

Meanwhile there was the Pastoral Measure of 1968, which brought Synodical government reorganisation of the Church of England, which meant streamlining the administration of the Church, bigger deaneries and grouped parishes - the grouping, in particular, "was quite a serious shock to the system, not just for the laity but for the clergy", in the words of Michael Sayer, a founder member of The Norfolk Churches Trust with Lady Harrod.

Nonetheless, carried along by the prevailing trend of the moment, there were people trotting off to the Synods with the thought that they would close unwanted churches to save expense, as Richard Butler-Stoney, another Trust founder member, wryly comments: "But they always sought to close somebody else's church, not their own!"

Convinced that it was vitally important to show to people, and to interpret to them, just what a treasure Norfolk has in its country churches, Richard began to organise church tours. The very first one attracted more than 100 people. The idea flourished, and in 2001 the tours are going as strong as ever.

"In 1972 there was a quite ordinary tour, when we went to a ruined church at Kempston, next to Litcham", Richard remembers. "From there we went on to West Lexham church, which was immaculate and a delight to everybody."

Among the crowd, again about 100 strong, was Lady Harrod. She was strongly impressed with the contrast between these two places. Both were villages with just one farm and its cottages, and the church. "She went home and formed the Committee for Country Churches, and I was among those she invited to join it."

Initially the new body worked under the wing of the Norfolk Society (the county branch of the Council for the Protection of Rural England). In 1976 it was re-founded as The Norfolk Churches Trust.

Initially it had its home in a room at Lady Harrod's house. During the time when Nicholas Corbin was Secretary in the early '80s, the HQ was moved to small rented rooms in Aylsham, and expenses kept to an absolute minimum. But basic furniture was needed, and Nicholas acquired a desk, a filing cabinet and a typist's chair, all second hand, for the princely sum of £126.50.

It was enough for a Council of Management member to record his disquiet at the fact that they were now spending £1000 per annum on rent, rates, electricity and general expenses, having previously managed in free accommodation.

The Secretary suggested that this was "an unrealistic point of view" - and the Council backed him!

From the start, the Trust's message was unequivocal - that churches don't have to be closed. Particularly fierce disapproval was voiced against the suggestion that redundant churches could be converted into private homes. "But this was one of the accepted ideas in the Pastoral Measure", says Lady Harrod. "I do think with all our propaganda we did turn things round."

Equally important was fund raising. If churches were to be helped when money needed to be spent, then the Trust had to have funds. "Money came in, in an amazing way," Lady Harrod relates. "We had an auction at King's Lynn and another at Banningham. We had only one appeal, which wasn't particularly successful. But the money rolled in nonetheless, and has continued to do so."

The biggest money raising event is the annual

A quarter century of rescues

During the 25 year life of The Norfolk Churches Trust, 25 churches have been rescued from closure, and even the possibility of demolition. After a period of disuse and decay, all are now re-opened for services of public worship, and can be visited.

Leased to the Trust are Cockthorpe, West Rudham, Dunton, Bagthorpe, Barmer, Hargham, Morton-on-the-Hill, Snetterton, Rackheath All Saints, West Bilney and Illington.

Helped by the Trust, and subsequently vested in the Redundant Churches Fund (now the Churches Conservation Trust) are Little Witchingham, Coston, Frenze and Thurgarton.

Corpusty has been helped by the Trust, and is now leased by the Friends of Friendless Churches.

Helped by the Trust and now maintained by Parochial Church Councils are Toftrees, Waterden, Southburgh, Whinburgh, Narford and Brandon Parva.

Helped by the NCT and subsequently maintained by parochial Trusts are Tunstall, Santon Warren and Rushmere.

bicycle ride, in which participants pedal to as many churches as they can in one day, and are sponsored by family and friends. The last event raised a staggering £107,000.

There are also Lady Harrod's long-running annual snowdrop mornings, coffee mornings with a difference, held in the garden of her home on the outskirts of Holt. The last one made over £3000.

In 1993 and '98, two very different events took place: Stately Car Boot Sales, the first at Houghton Hall, home of the Marquess of Cholmondely; the second at Holkham Hall, home of the Earl and Countess of Leicester. Attics were scoured at stately piles throughout the county, and to the vast pleasure of the Trust's present chairman, Charles Bingham-Newland, who master-minded both extravaganzas, the crowds flowed in – and so did the money.

Despite pouring rain, Houghton did handsomely. Holkham, with the sun on its side, did even better, bringing in £42,000. Now the wheels are turning for another Stately Car Boot Sale at Holkham Hall in May 2002.

In recent times a new equation has entered the fund-raising story. Under the Government's Landfill Tax Credit Scheme, WREN – the environmental body of Anti-Waste Ltd, a national but Norfolk-based waste management company – has over the past three years donated to the Trust a total of £250,000.

Going back to the 1970s, when the Trust first began, there was some suspicion of it among parishes and clergy. "A lot of people thought we were just preserving redundant churches", says Lady Harrod. "Once they realised what we were actually setting out to do, they were pleased."

The Trust put its aims into practice. Through the funds it raised, it was in a position to give practical financial help where it was needed. It was also able to give sound advice - and comfort and reassurance too, when church wardens and parishioners were in despair at how to deal with maintenance and repairs to the ancient church in their charge.

Then there was leadership by example - the Trust's celebrated working parties. It was Richard Butler-Stoney and his family who spearheaded this activity, and 25 years later continue to do so. Working parties had a simple objective: to move in, equipped with buckets and mops and scrubbing brushes, to clean up churches which had been allowed to slip into dilapidation and lack of care. "We went as volunteers to tidy them up, to remove the disgrace of vandalism in some places", Richard relates. "We stopped up holes in windows to prevent birds from getting in and making a mess. We repaired windows where we could. We tackled dirt generally, where parishioners had given up."

Almost always these activities had a very positive result. Local people came to see what they were

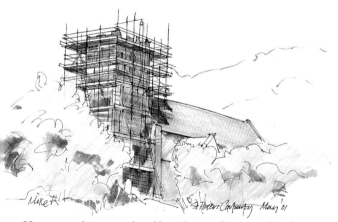

Urgent repairs currently taking place to Corpusty church
Drawing: Mike Fuggle

doing, were motivated by what they found, and many volunteered to help. The high point came when the "clean up" had been completed, and a service - invariably attracting large numbers of people - was held to celebrate the fact. It was the beginning of the turn of the wheel.

For Richard one of the most demanding, and rewarding, operations was Corpusty church,

which stands lonely on its hill looking down on Saxthorpe. It was in a terrible state, vandalised, pillaged and filthy. "The Friends of Friendless Churches rather despaired of the place. Then I heard on the grapevine that there was the possibility of its being turned into a house.

"I got local people to help me and we had working parties there - and how it needed it. We took out 17 wheelbarrow loads of bird muck, quite apart from other rubbish. When it was all done we had a service, which was well publicised, and many people came.

"The intention had been to hold the service in the open air. But it rained all that day, so the service went inside. It was absolutely packed to the doors. I'd taken along only a couple of collection bags, but they quickly filled and people had to lend their hats to be passed round. The collection brought in £400."

There are many similar stories to be told, when so many people gave their time and efforts to help pull a church back from the edge, and it was not unusual to see the Trust's founding lady down on her hands and knees, scrubbing pamments with the best of them.

In the early years, the diocese officially, from Bishop's House downwards, was less than enthusiastic. What the Trust was doing did not fit into the "rationalisation" doctrine of the moment.

But at the grass roots, the response was enthusiastic. This was particularly so, for example, at Cockthorpe, Bagthorpe and Dunton, in whose future the Trust was to play a key role. Then there was Wilby, south of Attleborough. "It was about to be closed but we fought a great battle with the diocese and we rescued it", Lady Harrod spiritedly recalls. "We had a wonderful triumph, and the people in the village were absolutely delighted." Activity by parishioners, encouraged by the Trust, had the same happy outcome at Mundford.

As the word spread at what the Trust was doing, support grew accordingly. There was pleasure in the villages when they were offered financial help, and relief that they would not have to spend an enormous amount of their own money. "The Archdeacons had told them they would not be able to have their own church, because they would have to raise all the money themselves." There was not a great deal of state grant aid available in the early 1970s, so it was all too easy for people to get depressed about the situation when restorations were necessary, says Michael Sayer. By the late '60s, he reminds us, a large number of country churches were "disused or tottering that way", but the Redundant Churches Fund (now the Churches Conservation Trust) rescued many of them.

"By picking up a lot of these churches, which were overwhelmingly medieval, it acted as a very real and important safety net. Here it was supplemented by the NCT and also by the Norwich Historic Churches Trust.

"In Norfolk there were 20 to 30 churches where it gradually became plain that they were little used or redundant. Some of these went to the Redundant Churches Fund. Others the Trust took over on long leases, beginning in the late '70s." Initially the responsibility was accepted for 10 churches, an eleventh being added later. (See panel within this article, headed *A quarter century of rescues*).

In all these cases, it was determined from the start, and still continues, that at least a few times every year, each church would have services, which never fail to attract eager congregations. This also provided a very practical spin-off.

In the 1980s, the Department of the Environment (now English Heritage) made repair grants available only to churches in use for regular worship. But because services were consistently held in the Trust's leased churches, the Department relaxed the rules and paid up! Within the parishes, there is recognition that, in Michael Sayer's words, "there has always been a loyalty to the building, as distinct from what goes on inside it - people who might not go regularly to worship, but who nevertheless will go at Christmas and Harvest Festival and the like. There have always been people who rally round

to help the building, even if they are not there on a Sunday to Sunday basis."

He suggests that one aspect which should be examined is the separation of the maintenance of the church building from the costs of maintenance of the ministry. "There is a tendency always in diocesan circles to wrap up the two together, which I think is not helpful." The writer of this article recalls a conversation with a Norfolk priest who had half a dozen medieval churches in his charge, and deeply resented the burden they placed upon him. "I am here for the cure of souls", he declared, "not for the cure of bricks and mortar."

Anthony Barnes, who served for three years as secretary of the Trust, has a crisp response: "If a vicar does not delegate, perhaps he has only himself to blame." He suggests that the answer could be to appoint a Fabric Officer, charged with leading the care of the church fabric. His main achievement as secretary, he suggests, was to change the mood regarding the whole issue of restoration and repairs. He made it his business to visit every church in the county. "So when everyone was saying, 'We are in a terrible crisis, all the churches are falling down and none of us can cope', I could say confidently: 'In fact an awful lot of our churches are in perfectly good order'. "It enabled me then to add: 'These are the ones we should be worrying about, where we must intervene and get something done if no action is being taken locally'."

Church wardens and parishioners were able to realise that they were not alone, and that when they had problems it was possible to tackle them in bite-size pieces. "We could tell them that there was a fair chance of support from English Heritage; that support would come also from the Trust; and the Historical Churches Preservation Trust might do likewise."

Improvements for the future?

Keeping churches open, accessible - and unlocked.
Installation of handrails and ramps.
Welcoming notices for visitors.
Supporting increased congregations.
Developing the use of local guides to interpret our churches.
Putting electric cables underground, and improving heating.
Measures to protect from lightning, vandals and thieves.
Providing nest boxes, bat boxes and owl holes.
Wildflower conservation in churchyards.
Making plans of graves in churchyards.
Improving car parks.

Compiled by Richard Butler-Stoney

In addition there was practical assistance, when Trust volunteers were prepared to come along to tidy up churchyards and lime-wash walls and the like.

"We have done this for many individual churches. We are simply saying: 'Here are 15 or 20 churches about which we are seriously concerned - but we are not worried seriously about the other 630'. And suddenly the whole thing becomes easier, and the Trust can focus attention on those really requiring help."

He notes that there are at this time about a dozen "living" churches for which there is concern for their future.

The eleven leased churches need an annual budget in the region of £20,000 to care for them. "Out of annual spending by the Trust of roughly £200,000, this isn't a lot. There are those within the Trust however who are not happy about that expenditure. But we had to rescue them, or let them rot."

Anthony points to West Rudham, one of the leased churches, as a happy justification of the Trust's policy. "It is run very much by a group of local people, who talk in terms of taking their church back into the diocesan system. This may not happen quickly, but they are doing the valuable task of keeping the church ticking over." He talks also of Illington, another leased building, where local people had lost heart. "But one thing the Trust does is to stop people being unhappy," Anthony beams. The building had been neglected for a long time. The Trust went to work and repaired the tower. The roof is in a bad way, but a scheme is in hand to put it right. Inside, some pews will need attention.

Objective: To put the church in good heart - and the local people too.

Within its lifetime, the Trust has saved not only its eleven leased churches, but has played a key role in rescuing 14 others (see panel within this essay, headed *A quarter century of rescues*): a grand total of 25 rescues in 25 years.

Anthony Barnes quotes examples of churches within the diocesan system which have received help and encouragement. Hassingham was little used, and was a strain on the parish of Strumpshaw next door. "So with our encouragement, a local Trust has been set up to take care of maintenance and repairs. A legacy was received a short time ago which will pay for repairs, so that is a happy story."

A few years back Michael Sayer was concerned that the sea would come in at Waxham and Sea Palling. "So very quickly," says Anthony, "we paid for the walls of both churches, where they were shaky, to be re-pointed up to sill level. It would have needed a lot of sea to knock them down after that."

Similar stories are legion. The signs county-wide are reassuring. Twenty five years on from the Trust's foundation, the climate of opinion in Norfolk has greatly changed. There is no more talk of having too many churches. Nor is there talk about redundancies. Alternative uses have been found to be a waste of time. And the diocese has re-adjusted to a policy of maintaining all its churches for worship, using lay help to balance a reduced workforce of clergy.

But within the Norfolk Churches Trust there is no complacency. The work goes on, looking forward to the next 25 years.

Burnham Norton Church. Watercolour by James Bulwer (attrib).
© Norwich Castle Museum and Art Gallery

Saxon? Norman? Or even later?

A debate that will run and run

For perhaps a century and a half, the reality of Saxon churches and, in East Anglia, their round towers, and their dating during the 150 years before the Norman Conquest of England in 1066, has been a generally accepted truth. But in recent years a new wave of scholarship has told us that virtually all these "Saxon" churches were in fact built after the Conquest and into the 15th century. Charles Roberts sets out the two cases.

THE POST-CONQUEST VIEW

It was in 1988 that Stephen Haywood, now Conservation Officer in Norfolk County Council's Building Conservation Centre, ran up the banner against "Saxon" churches in a paper for the Oxford University Committee for Archaeology.

The circular western tower, attached to a nave without aisles and to a chancel, is a common sight in the East Anglian landscape, he agreed.

Then in a withering paragraph he added: "The lack of parallels in other parts of Britain, and the use in some instances of archaic techniques of construction, have inspired local antiquarians to make romantic statements about the origins of the East Anglian round tower, and to claim extreme antiquity."

Romanticism

The full case he made then against this "romanticism" he reiterated in an article in the Norfolk Churches Trust annual report for 2000. The round western towers, he observes, range in date from the late 11th century to the 15th, of which by far the greatest majority belongs to the 12th century.

He notes the "strongly held belief" that the reason for the towers being round is due to the lack of suitable freestone in the region (where only flint is available), stone being necessary for making corners (quoins) needed for square or rectangular towers.

"As attractive as this theory might appear, it is wholly unreasonable when considered in the light of the many square towers without ashlar (dressed stone) quoins", and also nave corners without quoin stones. "As seductive as this practical explanation may at first appear, it is illogical and dull."

Early towers

Round towers, he continues, were a conscious choice - and probably copied from those in neighbouring villages. But from whom did they copy? Possibly, suggests Mr Heywood, from the round, radiating chapels at the east end of Herbert de Losinga's new cathedral at Norwich. If this is so, it "provides a terminus post quem of 1081 for the earliest East Anglian round towers" However, those earliest towers frequently have features and employ techniques which are associated with Anglo-Saxon Romanesque architecture. "The use of any one or several of these techniques are sometimes claimed as sure indications of Anglo-Saxon date." But it would be surprising, he suggests, "if these techniques did not survive into the 12th century".

Marvellous mix

He quotes examples of techniques used "in buildings of evidently post-Conquest date". He quotes the cases of Hales St Margaret, and Haddiscoe St Mary, whose bell openings "display a marvellous mixture of pre- and post-Conquest techniques". Many similar examples survived well into the middle years of the 12th century.

Three years ago, in an Eastern Daily Press article, Andrew Rogerson, Norfolk Landscape Archaeologist, expressed the view that: "We need more examples before we can be sure. But it seems likely that there were very few Norfolk churches built in stone before the Norman

Initial decoration: Brass of priest wearing full eucharistic vestments. Beachamwell St Mary

Conquest. Where Anglo-Saxon churches are found, they are invariably of timber, and their remains underlie the earliest phase of masonry building".

This opinion brought a sharp riposte from Bill Goode (see The Saxon view), who has been dubbed "The evangelist of East Anglia's Saxon churches".

THE SAXON VIEW

 Bill Goode entered late in life, and from scratch, the rarefied realm of research into Saxon round towers. But 17 intensely applied and minutely detailed years later, he emerged as an authority - as well as founder and life president of the Round Tower Churches Society; and author of a meticulously argued book, East Anglian Round Towers and their Churches.

In the book, he set out his stall briskly: "The round towers were built after the Vikings had settled in East Anglia, often as additions to existing churches. The upper doorways" (triangular headed, at "first floor level", looking down into the interior of the church from the east side of the tower) "were simply the entrance to an upper room.

"The tower arch of flints or rubble, i.e. without the use of dressed stone, confirms that it is of pre-conquest date.

Summoning bells

"The position of a round tower is no more important than that of any other medieval church … This is not to say that they have never been utilised at lookouts, as most churches have been used in this way at some time. But their prime purpose in being built was to hang church bells to summon the faithful to Mass and other celebrations."

As a clincher, he includes in chapter one the fact that King Athelstan made a law in 937, that "a Bell Tower should be built on the land of every Thegn".

"Before a law such as this could be made, there must have been bells in fairly common use, and towers must have existed, even if not very tall."

Lot to learn

He was quick to take up archaeologist Andrew Rogerson's assertion in the Eastern Daily Press in 1998 (see final paragraphs in The post-Conquest view) that there were very few churches built in stone before the Norman invasion. "If he needs more examples before he can be sure, then he still has a lot to learn," wrote Mr Goode tartly.

"While all the early churches were probably of wood, they would certainly have been replaced by stone at the earliest opportunity. This was 300 years before the Conquest, yet we are asked to believe that no, or few, stone churches were built in that period, while hundreds were built in the 100 years of the Norman period.

"Although Mr Rogerson and other archaeologists may maintain that the many flint churches of Norfolk were in fact built after the Conquest, no one has so far proved that one of these Saxon features is post-Conquest."

Proper job

If none or very few Saxon churches were built in Norfolk before the Conquest, where, he demands, do the Saxon features in stone come from? How did they originate? And if Mr Rogerson and his colleagues are right, why should the Normans build such fine doorways with masses of excellent stone - yet in the same building construct windows and corners with flint, when they had the stone to do the job properly?

After 1066 the Norman influence on church architecture becomes obvious, he points out. However, many churches and towers attributed entirely to Norman builders, were in fact Saxon, "modernised" to more sophisticated Norman taste by the insertion of windows, doorways and corner stones in fine dressed and carved stone.

He and his book, containing all his researches, are adamant: Of the round towers listed and surveyed, 75 per cent are proved to be pre-Conquest!

A flame that lasted a lifetime

In the early 1970s, the embryo Norfolk Churches Trust (then part of the Norfolk Society) issued its first publication. It contained an inspirational foreword by Sir John Betjeman. In a happy continuance of that link, Sir John's daughter Candida Lycett Green here reflects on a shared love of Norfolk churches.

As a child my father, John Betjeman, used to come to the Norfolk Broads and the River Bure, sailing and rowing with his father. But it was another aspect of the county which was to enthral him all his life.

He explained in his commentary for the film, A Passion for Churches …

"I think it was the outline of the church tower of Belaugh against the sky which gave me a passion for churches; so that every church I've been past since I've wanted to stop and look in."

If the flame was lit then when he was eight years old, it was certainly fanned by Billa Harrod in the 1940s and '50s when we all used to stay with her family at Bayfield Brecks in sandy, gorsy, piny country above the Glaven valley. From there you could see the towers of Blakeney, Wiveton and Cley. On Saturday afternoons, the grown ups used to go "church crawling", which meant stopping and looking at every single church they passed.

Us children on the other hand, my brother Paul, Dominick and Henry Harrod and sometimes Ned Hamond, all violently anti anything old, used to walk two miles to the cinema in Holt. It wasn't until the Harrods moved to the Old Rectory there, with the cinema right on the doorstep, that my horizons began to broaden and the glory of Norfolk's churches was revealed to me.

One of my favourites is Booton near the small, mellow brick town of Reepham, along the dipping, well-hedged lane which leads to a sparse scattering of houses and the much pinnacled and wildly eccentric creation of the Revd. Whitwell Elwin.

If you look northwards towards the coast you get a spectacular view of perhaps the most beautiful churches in Norfolk - Salle and Cawston, their great towers rising majestically from this mild and gentle East Anglian landscape; Salle's from huge lonely arable fields, and the 14th century Cawston's from the huddling roofs of the little town.

Perhaps it was their inspirational glory in this particularly pretty bit of the county which led Whitwell Elwin to Booton, coupled with the fact that his uncle, Caleb, was already patron and rector there in the 1830s when Whitwell decided to take holy orders.

Booton's houses and church evoke a perfect vignette of Victorian ecclesiastical life, centring around the magnetic character of its incumbent

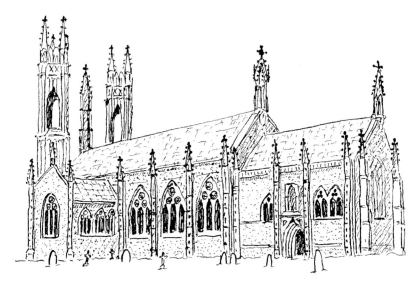

Booton church, entirely remodelled in the Victorian period by its remarkable rector, The Revd Whitwell Elwin.
Drawing: Hugh Holbeach

who was a direct descendant of Pocahontas, the native American princess who married an Englishman and died at Gravesend. Elwin's noble profile bore witness to this.

Initial decoration: Canopy of piscina with figures of a Woodwose (wildman) and a dragon developed from the heraldic symbols of the de la Poles and the Bedingfelds. Cawston St Agnes

He designed Booton as a complete amateur and took many of the features of the churches and cathedrals he had visited over the years, including Lichfield Cathedral, Temple Balsall in Warwickshire, St Stephen's Chapel at Westminster and Glastonbury Abbey.

Although Booton hasn't got a tower, it tells a story of faith - something my father never found easy to sustain. I think Norfolk's churches particularly gave him an extra strength which helped to quell his doubts:

What would you be, you wide East Anglian sky,
Without church towers to recognise you by?
What centuries of faith, in flint and stone,
Wait in this watery landscape, all alone.
To antiquaries, 'object of research',
To the bored tourist 'just another church'.
But still the faith of centuries is seen,
In those who walk to church across the green.
The faith of centuries is in the sound
Of Easter bells, that ring all Norfolk round.
And though for church we may not seem to care,
It's deeply part of us. Thank God it's there.

A priceless legacy

Norfolk's churches are a priceless architectural legacy. But they form a crucial part of the rural landscape. Their sheer numbers, and the idiosyncrasies of their location, are among the principal factors which give Norfolk's countryside its peculiar character: a character born of its own, very distinctive history.

Dr Tom Williamson, Lecturer in Landscape Archaeology, University of East Anglia

Picture: Salthouse St Nicholas. Photo: Richard Tilbrook

Finding the money – 25 years on

Sustained fund raising by the Norfolk Churches Trust, since its foundation 25 years ago, has been remarkably successful. Dominick Harrod, son of the Trust's founder, Lady Harrod – and former BBC Economics Editor - looks at the changing face of … Finding the Money.

Almost thirty years ago, I contributed an article to a publication called Norfolk Country Churches and the Future entitled Finding the Money. Thus we began the crusade of which we celebrate the twenty-fifth anniversary this year.

If we had then guessed how much money we would need, and would spend, we might have quailed. In that first review we touched on two elements which remain vital to the Trust's operations: the small scale things people can do to help themselves, and larger efforts needed to meet great challenges.

At the modest end of the scale, I wrote of St Margaret's, Cley-next-the-Sea, generating an income of £200 in the holiday month of August alone by offering post-cards and a leaflet, and making a small charge for brass rubbing. In the same booklet, Sir Edmund Neville told the story of the raising of more than £50,000 by the village of Worstead, in the years 1964-72, which helped to secure the tower of that magnificent church. Worstead points a useful moral that efforts to raise money can produce non-financial benefits. In Worstead's case, it was the annual Worstead Festival, giving pleasure to thousands who enjoy the event and visit the church year by year.

Classic case

Perhaps the classic case of giving pleasure while raising money, has been the series of Bicycle Rides. The sponsored ride each September now generates £100,000 of which half goes to the individual church of the rider's choice; and the other half to the Norfolk Churches Trust. This encourages the entrant to choose a church dear to him or herself, as well as benefiting the whole Trust. The sponsors may in part be

On a bike ride made for two – Bishop Graham of Norwich and Dean Stephen Platten, setting a cheerful example

generous from an understandably human motive that the riders love earning their quid or so, by sustained effort at the handle bars!

The bicycle ride is the largest single event in the calendar; but by no means the sole source of funds. One of the most important roles of the Trust is to advise parishes, and to help secure grants from national grant giving bodies like the Historic Churches Preservation Trust (HCPT), and English Heritage.

The twenty-fifth birthday comes at a time of unprecedented bounty for the task. This arises from Government policy and the generosity of the local waste-disposal company, Anti-Waste Ltd. Under the rules, companies involved in waste disposal by way of landfill receive a generous tax credit on their business *provided the money is used for environmental improvement*. The Norfolk Churches Trust is deemed a proper recipient of the Landfill Tax monies, so long as the church concerned is within 10 miles of a landfill site. The Company concerned, Anti-Waste Ltd, formed WREN (Waste Recycling Environmental Ltd), and earmarked substantial sums to come to the Trust. No less than £200,000 was paid in 1999-2000, representing £100,000 a year for two years; and the scheme is to produce another £50,000 a year for 2001-2.

Substantial grants

In 1999-2000, the Trust was able to offer £118,500 in grants from the WREN fund to 25 churches (compared with £149,122 offered from the general resources of the Trust). While organising the grants and getting the work carried out, takes a great deal longer than receiving the donation from WREN, the impact of the scheme will run on in the years to come. Meanwhile, the Trust is well supported by local government; but perhaps in view of the exceptional WREN money, there has been a drop, from £52,450 in 1999 to £34,900 in 2000, in the grants from local authorities.

At the same time, the main central Government source of support for the Churches, English Heritage, is under constant pressure of demand for funds, and no conservation effort such as the Trust promotes can be certain of perpetual support at the high levels of the past few years. But if the impact of official policy may be variable year by year, and budget by budget, there is also good news.

The Government's Gift Aid scheme, allowing the recovery of income tax on donations, will increase by thousands of pounds the value of individual contributions to the Trust.

Prosperity

On the whole, the present picture is one of an underlying prosperity. The Trust annual income of more than £200,000 (excluding the WREN money) includes £50,000 from the bicycle rides, and nearly £50,000 from interest on funds awaiting spending on Trust projects.

In recent years there have been very successful Trust activities like car boot sales and garden openings. And all these things require the continued, sustained voluntary efforts which have powered the Trust in the last 25 years.

But success has not led to complacency, and the Council of the Trust decided last year to increase the ordinary subscription from £10 to £20 from 2001. Membership fees accounted last year for

Peter de Bunsen and former Bishop of Norwich the Rt. Revd. Peter Nott with Derek Shepherd (Managing Director of Waste Recycling Environmental Ltd)

£16,000 out of £210,832 income (net of WREN money).

Membership, though contributing a modest share of total income, remains extremely important by encouraging us all to continue to support the activities and work of the Trust.

King's Lynn St Margaret, one of the churches benefitting from the WREN donation (see pages 10 and 23). Photo: Richard Tilbrook

King's Lynn Deanery
St John the Evangelist
○St Margaret with St Edmund
South Lynn All Saints

Norwich (East) Deanery
St Andrew
St George Colegate
St George Tombland
St Giles
St Helen
St John Timberhill with St Julian
St Mary-in-the-Marsh
St Peter Mancroft
St Stephen
Heartsease St Francis
Lakenham St Alban
Lakenham St Mark
Lakenham St John the Baptist
 & All Saints
Tuxford St Paul
Thorpe St Matthew
Thorpe Episcopi St Andrew
Trowse St Andrew

Norwich (North) Deanery
St Mary Magdalene with
 St James
Old Catton St Margaret
New Catton Christ Church
New Catton St Luke with
 St Augustine

Norwich (South) Deanery
Bowthorpe St Michael
Costessey St Edmund with
 St Helen
Earlham St Ann
Earlham St Elizabeth
Earlham St Mary
Eaton St Andrew with Christ
Heigham Holy Trinity
Heigham St Barnabas
Heigham St Thomas

Parishes in the Diocese of Ely

Fincham Deanery
Barton Bendish
○Beachamwell
Bexwell
Boughton
Crimplesham
Denver
Downham Market
○Fincham
Hilgay with Ten Mile Bank
Marham
Nordelph
Runcton Holme
Ryston
Shouldham
Shouldham Thorpe
South Runcton
Southery
Stow Bardolph
Stradsett
Tilney-cum-Islington
Tottenhill
Wallington
Watlington
○Wereham
West Dereham
Wimbotsham
Wormegay

Feltwell Deanery
○Feltwell
Hockwold-cum-Wilton
Methwold
Northwold
Weeting
Wittington
Wretton and Stoke Ferry

Fordham Deanery
Fordham

Lynn Marshland Deanery
Clenchwarton
Terrington St Clement
Terrington St John
Tilney All Saints
Tilney St Lawrence
Walpole St Peter with St Andrew
West Lynn
○West Walton
○Wiggenhall St Germans
Wiggenhall St Mary Magdelene

March Deanery
Welney

Wisbech Deanery
Emneth and Marshland St James
Outwell
Upwell St Peter
Walsoken

Their profusion

their greatness

Diocese of Norwich
revised 2001

*Originally prepared by The Society of St Luke
the Painter. Subsequently updated in the
Norwich Diocesan Office and reproduced here
with their permission*

KEY

Grants awarded by The NCT
✛ Parish Church
o Church in ruins or disused
✤ Church in Battle Area
▨ Urban areas
⚵ Redundant Churches
◯ WREN Churches

Parishes of Lowestoft
Christ Church
St Margaret
St Andrew

"The ointment in Norfolk's alabaster pot . . ."

Anthony Barnes was director of the Redundant Churches Fund in London (now the Churches Conservation Trust), before he came to this county and spent three years as Secretary of The Norfolk Churches Trust. He can claim the rare distinction of having visited every medieval church in Norfolk ... all 659 of them.

Probably the first image that comes to mind at the word "church" is of a calendar or Christmas card. It is a peaceful scene, superficially unchanged for decades, if not centuries. The church might be Hales with its Norman arches or Heydon at the end of its film-set village. There may be cows or sheep in the foreground or duck, if it's Wood Dalling. This serene picture conceals much of what actually has gone on. The fierce religious disagreements of the sixteenth and seventeenth centuries led to the destruction of statues, stained glass and wall-paintings, and sometimes to their concealment.

In recent years at Little Witchingham the battered remains of a scheme of wall-paintings has been discovered under protecting lime-wash. There may be as much to be found at Great Hockham. At Thorpe Abbotts priest or parishioners saved the carvings on the font from the image-breakers by plastering them over. They were not that old then, so when they were rediscovered by the vicar in 1840 and the plaster chipped away, they looked, and still do, almost brand new.

Remote churches

In many places churches are remote from their villages, often because the closure of fields and common lands provided better pasture for the sheep whose wool brought so much prosperity to Norfolk. Another cause may well have been the Black Death of 1349, though there is little hard evidence that this was so.

The Little Witchingham scheme is incomplete above the arcade, but the wall had been prepared for painting. Perhaps it was the money that ran out, but more likely it was life itself, extinguished by the terrible plague.

It was vandalism at that church that led to its repair and rescue by the Revd. Thomas Jeans in 1793 - without finding the wall-paintings. Wallington church did not survive Judge Gawdy's using it as a stable and hayloft in the early seventeenth century. In other places aisles built to cope with growing congregations in the late Middle Ages were pulled down, roofs were allowed to fall in and the present pattern of some ninety ruins was well established by 1800. The last unroofing was at Islington in 1972 after the lead was stolen.

Many people accuse the Victorians of vandalism, but their restorations often rescued buildings that had been neglected for a century. At their best - at Ickburgh or Glandford for example - they created virtually new buildings which would be a credit to any age.

Box pews

Even more precious, perhaps, are the churches where the money did not run so far, or where respect for what had been inherited stayed the hand of the restorer. So we have the box pews at Bylaugh, Thurning, Wilby and others; and the even older benches at the Wiggenhalls with their wonderful carvings; the furnishings at Beeston-next-Mileham or Burnham Norton; and so many more.

The most powerful assault on these buildings since the seventeenth century is the most recent. A long period of neglect has led in recent years to large repair bills for many churches. This has coincided with a conviction among many clergy and lay people that worship does not need to take place in special buildings. At the same time the number of people with a call to the ministry declined and the capacity of the church to pay the conventional number of priests ran out. The buildings came to be seen by many as an

Initial decoration: The original door in the tower of 1470, still in use today. Heydon St Peter and St Paul

intolerable burden, an impediment to the ministry. This was the context in which the Norfolk Churches Trust came into existence. During the last three decades much has changed. Individuals' generosity with their money and their time, massively supported by state aid to churches (a measure brought to Parliament largely through the conviction of Vivian Lipman, an observant Jew), has radically improved the churches' condition.

Enduring symbols

Churches have come to be seen as the enduring symbol of the communities in which they are set and are treasured as such by people who rarely, if ever, worship in them - but are fiercely protective and will often rally round to help with repairs. In this sense it is through its buildings that the Church can communicate to some of those outside it. This can be overlooked by ecclesiastical bureaucrats, schooled by decades of dwindling numbers and in whom has died the sense that the Church can have a mission. It also needs to be remembered that Norfolk's

population is growing, particularly with people of an age to take the place of the ageing stalwarts of the past. Demography is on the side of Norfolk's churches. It is far too early to give rural communities the additional pain of closing a church they love and where their representatives worship. It is not the buildings but the other paraphernalia of church-going that put off the non-attenders.

"Peaceful" is the word most often found in church visitors' books. A cliche perhaps, but indicative of a felt need. What may be being recognised here is the peace sometimes attained by an older person who has been through much. If so, we cannot have too many of such places. Perhaps Norfolk's logically unjustifiable number of village churches is its particular gift to the English community. The Gospel tells how the disciples were shocked by the waste when Mary Magdalene poured an alabaster pot of ointment of spikenard over Jesus's feet, and how He blessed her for what she had done. Norfolk's churches may be the ointment in our alabaster pot.

Bylaugh St Mary the Virgin. In 1809 box pews and three-decker pulpit were installed in the Prayer Book tradition.
Photo: Richard Tilbrook

A natural home for all - The next challenge?

Former editor of the Evening Standard *and* The Times, *and for five years deputy chairman of English Heritage, Simon Jenkins is also an immensely authoritative enthusiast for medieval churches. In 1999 he published* England's Thousand Best Churches, *a stimulating and splendidly opinionated book which took ten years to research and write. In this article he surveys Norfolk's churches, their cumulative heritage - and poses a challenge to their developing use in the future.*

No county in England is so defined by its churches as Norfolk. Their towers stride across its flat, silent landscape as sentinels of its past. That past, tempestuous under the Saxons and prosperous under the Normans, rose to a peak of wealth from wool cloth in the 14th and 15th centuries. In the decades before the Reformation, it produced buildings of stupendous size and richness.

Those who made their fortunes from wool poured much of it into their local churches, personal piety mingled with civic pride in a burst of patronage comparable only to that seen in the limestone belt of Gloucestershire and Somerset. The churches of Norfolk are customarily those of this last period of Gothic prosperity, known as Perpendicular. The county is rich in earlier works, in the round towers and Saxon/Norman foundations of Hales and Little Snoring and the florid Decorated tracery of Great Walsingham, Cley and Snettisham. But these pale alongside the frenzy of building that seized the county - and many others benefiting from the wool trade - after the Black Death and into the 15th century.

Mighty naves

The mighty naves and towers of Salle, Cawston, Wymondham and St Peter Mancroft in Norwich, must have been the biggest structures in England after the cathedrals. Rich men, no longer concerned with defending their property and their trade against marauders, could devote their money to guarding their reputation with their fellow citizens, and ultimately with God.

This created churches of the most spectacular generosity. Only today has the cost of redemption through building sponsorship become as widespread, albeit to the benefit of the arts rather than religion.

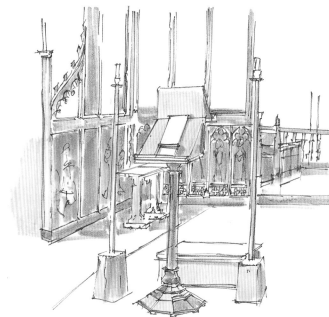

Rare Cantor's desk (precentor's lectern) and screen. Ranworth St Helen.

Cawston St Agnes. Drawings: Mike Fuggle

Initial decoration: Volute capital supporting a semi-circular arch with typical zig-zag decoration. Norman doorway, Brettenham St Andrew

It is hard to recreate the splendour of these late-medieval churches. The Reformation stripped away much of their colour and detail, later iconoclasm and neglect stripping away even more. We see traces of what must have been a glorious ceremonial at Walpole St Peter, in the screens at Ranworth and Worstead, and the fonts at Terrington and Trunch.

But to bring alive the vitality of these places, their guilds, societies and rituals, we have to go abroad, to the Easter festivals of Spain or the Venetian paintings of Carpaccio.

Ghosts of stone

What we lost in the upheavals of the 16th century we gained only in the absence of the later and more destructive upheavals which convulsed churches throughout Continental Europe. We may see only ghosts of what was left by the late Middle Ages, but at least those ghosts are of stone, flint, wood and glass.

I have often argued over the ranking of Norfolk's churches in what might be termed the English medieval cannon. What they boast in majesty and ubiquity they lack in subtlety of decoration and contents. Most are of flint, not the most tractable of materials.

The towers are undeniably big, but they lack the refinement of Somerset's towers or the sculptural quality of those of the East Midlands. They are not rich in architectural detail and the prevailing Perpendicular can seem monotonous after a long day of visiting. What is built for show is seldom built for artistry. Norfolk's churches can become a little dull.

But this is to quibble. We can only salute a county that sets out its historical stall so impressively. Nowhere in Europe can have so many massive structures of the pre-Renaissance period in such multitude. Some are struggling to stay aloft. But I was surprised at the good condition of so many, testament to the affection and energy lavished on them over the past quarter century.

A church in the Diocese of Norwich being demolished in 1977

Doomed

After the last war it was widely assumed that most of these buildings were doomed, as were many of the medieval churches in poor Norwich. This has not proved the case. By hook, crook, and grant, roofs have been repaired, windows reglazed and pews restored. These churches will be with us in some form for ever.

But in what form? What churches must find are new uses beyond that of irregular Anglican worship. An empty building is never wholly safe. A church without a lively congregation is a target for vandalism and renewed decay.

I still find it extraordinary that other Christian groups are excluded from using the principle Christian building of their parish, or are not actively encouraged to use it. I find it astonishing that every parochial activity, educational as well as artistic, is not directed to the church as its natural home.

These buildings were erected with the tithes and taxes, the craftsmanship and commitment, of the whole community. They belong to that community, in all its manifestations, and should be used to the full. That is the next challenge.

Stencil decoration from chancel of Hargham All Saints

Picture gallery

Southburgh Church 1848. Brown wash drawing by A. Rolfe. © Norwich Castle Museum and Art Gallery

West Bilney Church 1848. Brown wash drawing by A. Rolfe. © Norwich Castle Museum and Art Gallery

In the past, churches have been and still are a favourite subject for artists and photographers of all standards and abilities, as can be seen in the pages of this book. It is interesting to note that in some of the earlier pictures the condition of the churches is seen to be much worse than is the case today. In fact according to the last Bishop of Norwich, Bishop Peter, our Norfolk churches at the beginning of the 21st century are in the best condition they have been since the reign of Elizabeth I.

West Rudham Church 1849. Watercolour by James Bulwer (attrib). © Norwich Castle Museum and Art Gallery

North Barningham Church 1847. Watercolour by James Bulwer. © Norwich Castle Museum and Art Gallery

In praise of a pattern of songs in stone

Today's pattern of grouped parishes in rural Norfolk, often with a scattered gaggle of medieval churches, can be a burden - but a joy as well. Ian Whittle is Rector of Ashwicken with Leziate and Bawsey; Vicar of East Winch with West Bilney; Vicar of East Walton; Vicar of Gayton; and Rector of Gayton Thorpe. He is also a Chaplain to The Norfolk Churches Trust. He offers some thoughts on the rural experience.

"I don't think clerical poverty will suit you, darling . . " said my first prospective mother-in-law almost twenty years ago. "It will certainly not suit my daughter." She was right on both counts.

"And yet," said the late Bishop Aubrey Aitken, when I told him about it, "you might prove useful to somebody somewhere." And that swung it. Norwich professional life was exchanged for a state of seemingly permanent change: two years' voluntary work, three years of training and three more as a curate; six as a chaplain abroad; and at last, back to Norfolk.

With that came a rectory which scored one of my rare moral victories over my father: "And I thought you were in it for a decent house and garden, and not much to do."

The churches, though, are my delight. One, perhaps the finest, is kept locked, but four of them are always open. They are not just sermons in stone. They are songs!

Two others can not be other than open, being ruins. And one, the simplest, is in the care of the Norfolk Churches Trust. Saved from ruin, still a focus of parish pride and loyalty, it evokes our proper response to Almighty God. The building, given to divine service, requests and requires to be used for worship, prayers and preaching. Restored and maintained by determined guardians, this little church brings to mind what we've had; what we've lost; and what we might keep. It speaks of the fruitful balance of utility and beauty. For it might well have fallen down. It might have been sold. But its saving preserves this local gate to eternity.

Served and saved

Plainly the Church of God is the people of God, using some of the loveliest buildings on earth. These are places which echo the lives of those who have gone before … an echo which might help direct our future.

We owe a great deal to the men and women who have served and saved our Norfolk churches over the last twenty five years. I myself have been warmed by their delightful determination and cheerful giving, in the course of my living here, on and off, for the last two decades.

Perhaps every age is, in both senses of the phrase, a critical age; and the church, though often criticized, also acts as commentator on our times. Rumer Godden responded some years ago to criticism of Mother Theresa: "It is so easy to denigrate, so difficult to achieve." I take that very much to heart, both to govern my own way of dealing with others, and to help me deal with my own sense of cheerful failure.

So what, the critical reader may ask, do you actually do?

It may seem a funny place to begin, but one of my chief aims is to make the Rectory a useful and pleasant place, where parishioners know they will be welcomed. And so I feed and water as many individuals and groups as I can, though rather miss the entertainment allowance which I enjoyed in my last post.

Simple Y-tracery windows, typical of c.1300. Gayton Thorpe St Nicholas. Drawing: Hugh Holbeach

Initial decoration: 600 years old door knocker. Alderford St John the Baptist

The parishes have responded warmly; and I, in turn, am welcomed into so many peoples' houses. The more obvious part of work is public worship, and our pattern is, on Sunday, a Prayer Book Holy Communion at nine o' clock, and two, usually Morning Prayer services at eleven. We pop in a service with the Sunday School, and occasionally something in the evening.

Some would like more united services, but many of our seventy regulars don't bother to come. A recently formed choir adds a bit of spice.

Social mix

Drinks after some services have encouraged people to mix socially - sometimes for the first time ever. My wine merchant must think I live on sherry! Entertaining is, I think, as well as prayer and preaching and taking care of people, a key to the building up of our common life. Garden parties, supper parties, coffee mornings and lots of teas have been successful in attracting what some regard as "outsiders", as well as giving "insiders" practice in being welcoming.

In the same vein I go to as many village events as I can, including parish councils and societies. I sit on nine committees of charities and so on; and we have three church schools and five PCCs.

As for visiting, I see everyone I know to be ill or in hospital, unless they are attenders of other churches; and I aim to see newcomers and to do as much general visiting as time, patience and stamina allow.

I'd love to get around on a horse. But he'd have to live in the garage, and my bike gives me almost as much exercise.

Preaching I take seriously and find preparations and delivery both challenging and satisfying. Generally I speak for half the time I did in my last job, though sometimes they get the full dose; and more than once I've been told: "If you want lunch, watch the time." I do, and I don't.

Best friend

I pray, I suppose, at all times, but do so properly, mornings and most evenings, and use a variety of forms, though the Prayer Book is ever my best friend.

But the persisting glory of the Church of England is that prayer, life, work, hopes, regrets, parish, home, past, present and future, are all jumbled up together. And I've given up the

attempt to order them.

That doesn't mean there's no achievements. Marc Chagall wrote: "If you create from the heart, nearly everything works; if from the head, almost nothing."

So what about all the gaps, and the frustrations and the sense of being a very small bit of butter to spread over an awful lot of bread? I know that margarine would go further, but that's not the point. Nor do I like it.

If we are still on God's side, He must surely be on ours; and in Him there is completeness.

Walking round the garden with Nellie, one of my helps, she asked:

"... 'ere, what's that?"

" A dead bit of yew," I said.

"There ain't no bit o' me missin'," was her triumphant riposte.

I wonder what my fierce forebears (Vikings who 1100 years ago turned up on the East Anglian coast to steal and destroy) would make of me, having made a home here? Here where I find delight and satisfaction in my small involvement in this great work of keeping safe the treasure which is given to us. A treasure, moreover which is the best of the past for the service of the present, in trust for the future.

They might, perhaps, discover amazing riches in seeming clerical poverty.

Gayton Thorpe St Mary. Drawing: Hugh Holbeach

Joyful parties for the working day

Twenty-five years ago Richard Butler-Stoney was a founder of the Norfolk Churches Trust - and founder too of an institution which has throughout been a vital part of the Trust's work. That is, the working parties who - armed with buckets, mops, scrubbing brushes and all - descend cheerfully on neglected churches, and wash and polish them back to life. Here he reflects on a quarter century of faith and elbow grease!

Norfolk's church ruins arouse nostalgia for a past when the country side was teeming with families, busy producing their own food from farming, and living around a village green dominated by their village church.

A church going to ruin in our own generation arouses a deep sadness which causes some people to go away muttering expressions of blame; others stay away with a sense of shame; but yet others feel that it is a cry for help and a challenge to one's Christian loyalty.

Norfolk Churches Trust seeks to help where the need is greatest, and in its early years this meant going to help in desperate cases where pigeons had gained possession and ivy blocked the gutters.

The first step was always to fix a date for the working party of volunteers; after that the enthusiasm would start to build up. Birds inside a church can frustrate the cleaners beyond endurance, and so in the early days windows had to be patched with polycarbonate sheets to keep out pigeons, and mortar put under the eaves where sparrows delight to penetrate.

Scrub and polish

Meanwhile others would scrub and polish inside, and outside there might be ivy to remove, elder bushes to grub out and gutters to clean.

A picnic in the churchyard, or porch, always proved to be a happy social occasion, but the greatest joy was to see the church sparkling with smiles at the end of a good day's work. No such day was ever wasted; some churches responded immediately, and others took years to come back to regular worship, but they all came back in the end.

Bagthorpe Church was so bad that the church authorities took away its Norman font to a museum in Norwich. Great was the rejoicing when it was returned, and still more rejoicing when it was used to baptise a baby girl, who has been faithful at services ever since.

Norman font returned to Bagthorpe church to great rejoicing. Drawing: Rosamond Butler-Stoney

A working party cannot spend a day in a country church, no matter how remote, without someone local coming round to see what is going on. They see that if people from elsewhere care enough to restore the building, then it must be worthwhile for them to join in and help their own church. From this point enthusiasm grows and the church revives.

Great discovery

Ivy thrives on flint walls; it can get a root-hold in the lime mortar, so it is best removed while it is still green. When we removed the thick ivy from Coston church we discovered a wonderful 13th century Early English church in miniature, which was so good that it was saved from conversion into a house and qualified for conservation with national money. At Kempstone a double splayed window frame, typical of the Saxon period, had been hidden by ivy for 50 years.

Faithful church cleaners can be daunted by work on the tower, or by tall windows. A cry for help came from a small village where feathers had been noted in their vestry under the tower. A working party investigated - and discovered 40 pigeons in the belfry. By the end of the day the tower had been made bird proof and cleaned up. Lime washing and scrubbing the vestry was done on another day.

Windows used to need a lot of repair, but now the lead glaziers have caught up with this restoration work. If ventilation is poor, algae can grow on the inside of the glass. When the glass is washed with clean water, it transforms the beauty of the church.

Floors of our medieval churches are normally brick or pamments; the soil moisture passes through them to evaporate on the surface. With the passing of many years this evaporation leaves a residue of lime and salt to discolour the clay. Vigorous scrubbing will restore the attractive red and yellow brick colours. Some resort to carpets, but they are not appropriate; they spoil the acoustics and the rising damp soon rots them.

Baltic seed

Elder bushes grow fast and can quickly whip against walls and even windows. So they must be eliminated. One writer to the Press bemoaned a mass of seedling elder in Anmer churchyard, foretelling doom. She did not know of the rare plant, called Impatiens parviflora, which has a leaf like elder, but grows only one foot high. It came there 100 years ago as seed on the bark of pine trees from the Russian Baltic, which were used to roof the chancel.

After 25 years of working parties the pioneering work is nearly complete, but there is still great

need to answer cries for help in remote places. Lime washing the walls has become a major activity. It is important to use the correct material for church walls, and the result can be most uplifting. Traces of medieval wall painting are sometimes discovered to add to our understanding of the past. The outer arch of Tittleshall's porch had long been whitewashed over, but when cleaned down, the initials, mason's mark and date of a 17th century repairer were revealed.

Above and top right: Working party in action at Anmer.
Photos courtesy Lynn News.

Every church depends on the loving care given freely for the glory of God, and such time is never lost.

These hallowed places shall endure

Since his memorable début in 1990 with Watercolour Sky, which took his native Norfolk as its backcloth, William Rivière has established himself as a respected and much praised novelist. Here, with typical lyricism, he draws on memories of childhood, and of the county which has remained close to his heart through all his years of travelling the world.

I remember a Norfolk carol service when I was still child enough to be made exceedingly nervous by having to stand up before the congregation and read to them that "They shall not hurt nor destroy in all my holy mountain," despite having been exhaustively rehearsed for this honour in the kitchen at home.

I remember a harvest thanksgiving during the preparations for which the sexton, who had fought on the Western Front nearly half a century before, sat on the porch bench and showed me how to bind a sheaf of wheat. But my parents also often took my brother and me to visit churches when no service was to be held. We went to favourites of theirs like Edingthorpe and Oxnead, and to Sloley and Tunstead and Paston, to ferret among the nettles for the graves of people we were descended from. We rubbed the lichen away from the lettering on their headstones to check when they'd been born, who they'd married and when they'd died. I got to know Morston church because one of my grandmothers had a house there. My other grandmother took me to Salhouse where my

Morston Church 10 July 1855. Watercolour by James Bulwer. © Norwich Castle Museum and Art Gallery

Initial decoration: Ornamental candle holder. Brandon Parva

grandfather was buried at the foot of the tower, and where, she explained to me, she was going to join him.

Holy places

I must still have been very young, because I found this notion perplexing. She took me to Ranworth where from the top of the church tower I remember looking out with her over the broad and the alder carr and the fen. And so when long afterward I came to write novels, this love of the holy places of my childhood seemed to take its place in them very naturally.

By then I had haunted churches in France, Italy, Greece, and in Burma, India, Sri Lanka and Malaysia too, and I'd grown to love temples of other religions also. I never doubted that the mystery and resonance of a beautiful Christian church went beyond Protestant, Catholic or Orthodox doctrines; or doubted that sanctity and peace of spirit may be found in all manner of shrines all over the world, those still used for the celebration of a rite or those fallen into decay.

No electricity

It's the sort of instinct I'd absorbed from my father on those afternoons when I'd ridden my pony beside his horse up the grassy path to Crostwight with its stumpy tower and commendable lack of electricity.

He'd talk about the different styles of Gothic; about the Church's historic importance as a patron of architects, painters, composers, master-builders, workers in stone, glass, metal; about the beauty of the liturgy; about the seemingly universal need for rituals to welcome the newly born, to wed lovers, to honour the dead and to propitiate the unknown . . . before switching back to how vital it was to keep our Norfolk churches in good repair, and not as some of them had been in past centuries, nave roofs gaping, chancels used as byres.

Because what mattered was not church attendance, or even the flourishing or decline of a religion in a country. What mattered - whatever kind of believer, half-believer or sceptic you were - was the preservation of these masterpieces that had been bequeathed to us.

Banded together

Years later when we'd be back at Crostwight, he now walking slowly and leaning on a stick, we'd rejoice that it had turned out that there were thousands of us all over the county who were happy to band together for the Norfolk Churches Trust. It has been, and will continue to be, a resounding success.

That the hallowed places of our countryside should endure: this seems to me the essence of it. We each have our own loyalties - but I keep walking back to the old paupers' graveyard beside what used to be Smallburgh workhouse, its nave formed not of stone but superb lime trees, and outlasting the injustices its nameless dead suffered.

Then there is magnificent Tunstead church; and beautiful Irstead by the river Ant, where in small congregations, and not always every Sunday of the month, it's been possible to have the use of some of the finest architecture and finest English our forefathers have left us. And perhaps best of all is to sail offshore and see our medieval flint towers lording it over the coast and the sea.

Guardians of the Land

Here the farm land came to an end, joined almost flush against scalloped summer sea. No more wheatfields, woods, villages. No more rivers snaking through water-meadows past headless windmills, down cascades of watermills where decayed wheels hadn't turned for years, past rushy banks over which sails apparently without hulls dragged themselves across lowlands apparently without water. No more churches standing over fens where grebe and bittern breed, where marsh harriers tilt over reedbeds, where old vessels along dykes sink at their moorings. No more churches secluded in oaks and alders by their staithes. Here churches were gaunt fortresses against gales; they reared exposed from the last salt-bitten acres. Where the few copses that survived were stunted, every tree's back bowed, shoulders craven, arms hunched to protect cowed head, for parish after parish the flint church towers stood four square, indomitably upright, guardians of the land, watchers of the sea.

From Watercolour Sky, *by William Rivière, published by Hodder & Stoughton in 1990.*

Happisburgh Church. Pencil and watercolour by James Bulwer. © Norwich Castle Museum and Art Gallery

On Lady Katherine Paston's Tomb at Oxnead

Sun set three hundred years,
Those marble shadows on the wall still stand,
Fixed by her husband's grief, and Stone's*
*   hand,*
Long–vanished skill, and wealth, and tears.

Outside her dilapidated
Church the usual June again transposes
The graveyard offals into grass and roses,
Beauty and corruption equated,

Balanced principles,
Whereby this white memento-mori *is*
Now mere memoria pulchritudinis,
New summer dappling her walls.

We're not the tomorrow, alas,
Of this lady's wish; her treasures scattered for
*   ever,*
Her mansion now green mounds beside the
*   river,*
Not a Paston left to wear her flesh …

And since we put the resurrection
Even of annual crops to chance,
Eternity of blood's no longer, as once,
Any man's confident possession.

We do with less than that:
The uncertain hope that someone not yet born
May saunter here on a remote June morning
To find the key under the mat.

Michael Rivière (1919 – 1997)

father of William Rivière, with whom he shares these pages

Lady Katharine Paston's Tomb
at Oxnead · MikeF April 2001

*Nicholas Stone, d. 1647, was the greatest English sculptor of his century, who became master mason to James I and to Charles I.

Characters in a quiet revolution

Andrew Anderson has been involved with the care of historic churches for 40 years, and was Surveyor of St Albans Cathedral from 1974 to 2000. He is an Honorary Consulting Architect to the Historic Churches Conservation Trust. Here, with the lightest of touches, he paints a gallery of characters who have contributed to the renaissance over the past quarter century of Norfolk's great heritage of medieval churches.

There are two meanings of the word 'revolution' when it comes to describing events. One implies the forcible overthrow of an established order. The other "any fundamental change or reversal of conditions". Well, there has certainly been that as far as Norfolk's churches are concerned in the last twenty five years, but it has all been done very politely.

No-one has been eliminated. Rather, what has been gently overthrown has been a culture, a mind-set, a way of looking at things. What the founders of the Trust had that others lacked was, supremely, a vision - a vision of what was possible, an insight at a time when it was fashionable for bright young Church of England clergymen to talk of old churches as "useless plant", a time when Boards of Finance could not sell off the family silver fast enough.

I remember Horsey Rectory going under the hammer for eighteen hundred pounds in the 1960s and the parsonage at Woodton following, complete with its paddock and orchard, for three thousand four hundred not long afterwards.

Smithereens

Captain Horace Firth had had enough of war by the time he took charge at the Diocesan Board of Finance offices in Norwich Cathedral Close; but his successor as DBF Secretary, James Haddock - an engaging retired Sapper colonel - was still full of fight and made no secret of his ambition to blow every church in the county to smithereens. His fingers would twitch and his eyes sparkle as he recounted his dream, and I would not have been surprised to discover that he carried a roll of detonator wire about in his pocket just in case it came in handy.

It is remarkable that so few churches were added to Norfolk's two hundred and fifty or so ruined ones, Panxworth being an exception; with Crownthorpe sold largely intact for reinvention as a house. I remember both churches shortly after their abandonment when all that was needed was the re-fixing of a few loose slates. At Panxworth the Bible was still open on the lectern and candles in their stands on the communion table.

That others like Rackheath escaped, is due to a handful of remarkable people who began to be observed entering and leaving the Old Rectory, Holt (home of Norfolk Churches Trust founder Lady Harrod, as it happens) regularly and in groups, who in time enlisted a wider circle of like-minded campaigners and crusaders for excellence.

Calibre

There were people like Rosemary Adams and Ben Stimpson at Salle. There were far-sighted Norfolk landowners willing to show what could be done with the churches on their estates, men of the calibre of Jim Neville at Sloley and Worstead.

Jim worshipped his Maker from the comfort of an armchair sent over from the Hall and had a mynah bird called Percy he taught to say "Blast Wilson" (it was the days of a Labour government). He wrote in a beautiful calligraphic script and had a fine way with words, although it did not always pay to be at the receiving end - his MC in the First World War was not awarded for sitting in the trenches.

The intrepid lay men and women on whom the Trust was built are rightly remembered and celebrated, but their efforts would have been much harder without the support and sympathy of a tenacious group of exceptional Norfolk clergymen and their wives. I think of people like Aubrey Aitken, later Bishop of Lynn, and Billa Harrod's unflinching ally in the Diocesan

Initial decoration: Jacobean pulpit 'sett uppe by Broadhead of Creeke' c.1655. North Barsham All Saints

Advisory Committee battles of the 1970s; and Hugh and Freda Blackburne, whom Launcelot Fleming brought from Harrow to set up and run the Hilborough Group, leading by example, and steadily repairing their ten churches one by one, with much patience and good humour. It is no surprise that Hugh's first curate, at Foulden, is now Bishop of Hereford.

Pig-keeper

Other heroes of the time were Oliver Rooke, the pig-keeping parson at Great Massingham and Harpley (a beautiful headache if ever there was one); Charles Shells, leader of the Trunch Group in the early days; fellow team leaders with clusters of churches like Peter Bradshaw at Hempnall, Peter Moss at Mattishall, and Julian Barker in the Raveningham Group.

Then there was Gerald Epps on the north escarpment of the lower Yare valley; Noel Boston, the intrepid antiquarian vicar of East Dereham in whose company you risked being deafened or shot (or both); and Reggie and Fiona Wylam at North Barsham where, if you were lucky, lunch was a trout caught in the river that morning. It is an impressive list.

Everyone's efforts, those of lay people and clergy alike, would have remained a dream, however, had it not been for the half dozen or so architects who, at a time when the bulldozers were rampant in city centres and country estates and money was to be made razing old buildings to the ground, saw Norfolk's churches as serious business.

These were professionals with the patience and dedication to rediscover lost building techniques - pioneers like Cecil Upcher who gave me his 1890 White's Directory of Norfolk when he finally retired aged 80 plus; Bernard Feilden, and Donovan Purcell, Bernard fathering a whole generation of church specialists.

Fortunate

And Norfolk has, I think, been fortunate in its home-bred craftsmen and women whom the architects found ready and waiting for the call to arms: Dennis King (glass), Eric Stevenson (ironwork), Joe Royal (font covers), John Sumner (lead), Donny Woods (stone), and Pauline Plummer (rood screens) to name but a few. There are the unrecorded, unsung battalions of

bricklayers, carpenters, roofers and plumbers commanded by the likes of Bob Carter, Bill Lusher and Jim Middleton, who have repointed towers, re-laid floors, replaced lead and slates on chancels and naves, and over the years, lime washed walls at little profit to themselves (I suspect).

Thanks to the Trust and its supporters and servants, Norfolk today is a countryside filled with living churches, a county that politicians' threats, foot and mouth, BSE, and the four and a half feet of rain we have had in the last twelve months, are powerless to destroy.

Splendid three-decker pulpit of Salle St Peter and St Paul.
Photo: Richard Tilbrook

An ever greater glory
The first 25 years of the Norfolk Churches Trust
Compiled by Richard Butler-Stoney

1968   To close churches, a procedure was laid down by the 1968 Pastoral Measure. A national organisation was set up to judge whether a redundant church was important enough to deserve preservation, and if not an alternative use had to be found by the Diocesan Alternative Uses Committee. Despite enthusiasm for alternative uses, this found no alternative for rural churches; in which case the Measure laid down that the church should be demolished. This aroused great anguish throughout Norfolk.

1969   Brooke Commission Report on Norwich city churches, resulting in the number of closed churches in the city centre increasing to 24 out of the 32 in the city.

1970   Establishment of synodical government with larger deaneries and more power given to the laity.

1971   Lady Harrod formed The Committee for Country Churches under the structure of The Norfolk Society. Frequent meetings were held in her house, where plans were worked out to save Norfolk churches.

1972   Publication of Norfolk Country Churches and the Future. This emphasised the importance and glory of Norfolk's village churches and the determination to keep and use them all for worship.

1973   The Sheffield Report to synods recommended drastic reduction of clergy in the countryside for the benefit of mission in towns.

1974   Publication of a further four books which extolled the marvels of our village churches in architecture, medieval stained glass, monuments and brasses.

1975   Leases negotiated to save Cockthorpe, Barmer and Dunton churches. Emergency repairs are carried out by local builders, and parties of volunteers work to heal the disgrace of neglected churches.

1976   Many fund raising events, including The Week's Good Cause, Garden Openings and exhibitions. Bagthorpe, Hargham and Morton-on-the-Hill leased.

1977   The start of State Aid Grants for historic churches.

Horningtoft saved from closure by re-roofing. Needlework Exhibition in Wymondham Abbey.

1978   Extensive publication of Church Guides by Simon Cotton and Richard Butler-Stoney, seeking to fill the gaps across the county. Snetterton Church leased. Snowdrop mornings at Holt and Open Days at Banningham become established events of great popularity.

1979   Working Parties helped to save Thurgarton and Coston churches, which enabled them to qualify for vesting in the Redundant Churches Fund. Snetterton church leased by the Trust. Hargham chancel re-roofed and restored.

1980   At Morton-on-the-Hill the round tower had collapsed on to the nave in 1959 and the church was abandoned. Working parties cleared the rubble and the surviving part was restored to an imaginative design. Emergency repairs by the Trust to Little Witchingham church, where exciting wall paintings were found.

1981   Grants amounting to £14,975 were awarded during this year from money raised voluntarily. Fire in the thatched roof of Reedham church.

1982   An Appeal was launched which established a firm foundation for the finances of the Trust. Panxworth nave and chancel were demolished under the 1968 Pastoral Measure Scheme.

1983   Working Parties continued at our leased churches, and also at Great Hautbois, Corpusty, Anmer and Tunstall. Contents removed from Forncett St Mary.

1984   The first sponsored Cycle Ride was organised when all churches were opened and manned on a Saturday, and cyclists of all ages were sponsored to ride to as many churches as possible. Half the money raised was immediately returned to the church of the cyclist's choice, and the rest used for grant-aid restoration work.

Small illustration: Detail from The Marcon Window depicting Canon Marcon on his cycle. Edgefield St Peter and St Paul

1985 Conference organised jointly with Norfolk County Council, entitled Churches at Risk. This dealt with problems in saving churches and led to researching and later conserving the most important ruins.

1986 Grants reached £52,400. Debate on St Benedict's belief that one is called to worship God where one actually is, and that means in one's own Parish Church. This led on to see how the building is the focus of parish life, expressing the universality of God's presence everywhere. In contrast a decayed church spells out a God-forsaken community.

1987 Advisory church visits greatly increased. Southburgh church supported temporarily to enable the combined P.C.C. to restore Cranworth church.

1988 HRH the Prince of Wales becomes Patron. Wall painting discovered in Cockthorpe. Exhibitions in West Rudham, Dunton, Barmer and Bagthorpe under the heading of "Four Churches Rejoice" to celebrate ten years with the Trust. The U.E.A. confers on Lady Harrod a Doctor of Civil Law honorary degree.

1989 West Bilney church tower is restored and a 21 year lease negotiated for upkeep of its church. Re-thatching of Mautby church and repairs to other neighbouring churches. Cycle Ride raised a record £78,900 for Norfolk churches and the idea spread across many other counties, resulting in £700,000 being raised nationally. One energetic father and son visited 43 churches on their cycles and raised £1,000 in spite of wind and rain that day! Exchange visit to the Old Churches around Groningen in The Netherlands. The International League for the Protection of Horses (ILPH) moves to Snetterton and staff come to their first Carol Service in Snetterton church.

1990 Whinburgh church restored. Start made on Runham church. The Blofeld Commission studies Rural Church Buildings for a report to the Bishop of Norwich.

1991 An Events List for the county is first published by the Trust. Lawrence Jones died leaving a legacy to the Trust. Return visit of the Stichling Oude Groningen Kirken. The round tower at Cockley Cley collapsed into a heap of rubble and flints.

1992 The first great autumn Plant Sale at Elsing Hall. Waterden restored. The Trust produces a response to the Diocesan Resources Working Party Report.

1993 The Trust's office moved to the Old Church in St Matthew's Road, Norwich after seven years in Aylsham. Among many important church restorations, Brisley and South Lopham are outstanding because they require continued support over several years. The secretary completed his visits to every church in Norfolk, 659 of them! The Stately Car Boot Sale at Houghton Hall raised £20,000 from items cleared from the attics of 70 of the larger houses in Norfolk.

1994 Carols by Candlelight in our leased churches.

1995 Advice given to certain parishes to set up Fabric Trusts, or a Friends organisation to finance repair work where there is a conflict over raising money for maintaining the ministry of the church.

1996 Illington church leased and its dangerous tower restored. Plant Sale at Sennowe Park raised about £20,000. Norfolk Churches Great & Small published with 186 colour pictures by Richard Tilbrook, and text by Charles Roberts.

1997 Stately car boot sale at Holkham Hall raised £42,000. Campaign started for reduction of VAT on church repairs; this took four years to achieve a concession.

1998 Landfill Tax brought substantial money for repair of churches. Working parties helped churches in special need. First service in Corpusty church since 1950s.

1999 Yew trees grown from cuttings off a tree 2000 years old were distributed from Norwich Cathedral for planting in churchyards throughout the Diocese, to celebrate the second millenium of Christianity.

2000 Record year for the Sponsored Cycle Ride which raised more than £100,000. Grants to churches doing restoration work also reached a record level of £268,000. Church tours continued on the same successful pattern - printed leaflets for 340 churches are now available.

Small illustrations: (Left) Bagthorpe St Mary the Virgin. (Right) Pricket light in Bircham Newton All Saints

An Inward and Spiritual Grace

With the appointment in 1977 of four volunteer chaplains, there came an important development in the work of The Norfolk Churches Trust.

These chaplains, who were either working priests or retired clergy, volunteered to take services in the churches which had come under the Trust's care.

Maurice Wood, the then Bishop of Norwich, presided over a simple service at St Peter's, Dunton, where the chaplains were welcomed into the ministry.

All there will remember the parable he recounted. He had, he said, recently carried out a Confirmation in just such a rural village as Dunton.

The vicar particularly asked the Bishop to take the Confirmation in the smallest and most remote of the three or four villages in his care.

Five out of the six candidates for confirmation were adults. What was remarkable was that they had all come forward for confirmation as a direct result of working with their hands to tidy up and then repair the churchyard and the church itself.

Bishop Maurice quoted the text of St Peter's first epistle, Chapter 2: "Ye also as lively stones, are built up a spiritual House …".

"By addressing themselves to the ancient stones of the church," said the Bishop, "they found the desire to become the living stones of the church of which St Peter wrote".

That sermon encapsulated a truth important to members of the Trust, that the fabric of the churches all around us is by no means separate from, or competing with, our personal faith. Rather, a visible church, in stone, wood and glass, is a great support to many of us in the invisible church of our faith.

Another Bishop of Norwich, Peter Nott, aptly summed up the position, saying the churches were for him Sacramental. That is, as the Catechism teaches, "an outward and visible sign of an inward and spiritual grace".

It is in that light, for the past quarter century, that they have been cherished by the Trust and its members.

Dominick Harrod

Who's Who in the Norfolk Churches Trust 2001

Patron	H.R.H. The Prince of Wales
Vice Patrons	The Duke of Norfolk
	The Bishop of Norwich
	The Bishop of Ely

Council of Management

President	Lady Harrod OBE
Vice President	Richard Butler-Stoney OBE
Chairman	Charles Bingham-Newland
Vice Chairman	Lady Egerton
Hon Treasurer	Maurice de Bunsen
Chairman Grants Committee	Michael Sayer
Bicycle Ride Organiser	Brian Iles
Secretary	Malcom Fisher

A Prayer for The Norfolk Churches Trust

Bless, O God, the work of the Norfolk Churches Trust in its concern for the parish churches of this county, that they may be preserved and enhanced as signs and channels of your abiding love and presence in every place, and serve as beacons of faith and hope to succeeding generations, through Jesus Christ, your son, our Lord. Amen.

This prayer was compiled by the Revd. Canon David Ainsworth, Hon. Chaplain to The NCT.
It is always used in the Trust's leased churches, and on many other occasions where the Trust has helped churches in need.

Acknowledgements

We are grateful to those whose generosity has helped to make this volume possible:

Bernard Matthews plc   John Jarrold Trust
Eastern Counties Newspapers   Porvair plc
The Lady Hinde Trust   Frederick Hiam Charitable Trust

We are also grateful to Richard Tilbrook who kindly agreed to the inclusion in this book, of some of his superb photographs, from *Norfolk's Churches Great and Small*, which have greatly enhanced this production.

The initial decorations punctuating articles in this anniversary book have been taken from the *Church Tours* leaflets compiled by Richard Butler-Stoney. Almost all have been drawn by Rosamond Butler-Stoney.

C V Roberts

Since his arrival in Norfolk in 1972, Charles Roberts, editor of this volume, has pursued a passion for medieval churches which began when he was a 15 year old in North Staffordshire. For 28 years, up to 1997, he held the post of Arts Editor of the *Eastern Daily Press*, where naturally he extended "the arts" to include the county's medieval churches. He began taking guided tours around these churches ten years ago, and still does so. His activities combined to bring him Fellowship of the Royal Society of Arts, 1990; the accolade of Britain's Best Regional Theatre Critic, 1991; and the Honorary Degree of Master of Arts from the University of East Anglia, 1993. He is co-author with D.P. Mortlock of the three-volume *Popular Guide to Norfolk Churches*; and wrote the text of *Norfolk's Churches Great and Small*, in partnership with the photographer Richard Tilbrook (1997).

Mike Fuggle

The designer of this volume, Mike Fuggle, spent his working life in printing, beginning at the age of 14 years as an apprentice compositor in the Jarrold print works. He progressed to the Design department, of which he eventually became head. Since retirement, having become hooked on medieval churches, he teamed up with the photographer Richard Tilbrook, helping with the practical aspects of Richard's exhibitions, *Churches in an East Anglian Landscape*. He came out of retirement to join Richard Tilbrook and Charles Roberts in the creation of *Norfolk's Churches Great and Small*; and has now joined Charles in bringing together this 25th anniversary book of The Norfolk Churches Trust

**The NORFOLK
CHURCHES TRUST**

**Registered Office: 9 The Old Church, St Matthews Road, Norwich NR1 1SP Tel: 01603 767576
Web: www.norfolk-churches.co.uk**
Registered Charity Number 271176   Environmental Body Number 111076
Registered Company Number 1247797